# GRAPHIC NONFICTION

# SITTING BULL

## THE LIFE OF A LAKOTA SIOUX CHIEF

*by*
**GARY JEFFREY & KATE PETTY**

*illustrated by*
**TERRY RILEY**

rosen central™

The Rosen Publishing Group, Inc., New York

Published in 2005 by The Rosen Publishing Group, Inc.
29 East 21st Street, New York, NY 10010

**First edition, 2005**

Designed and produced by
David West Books

*Editor:* Gail Bushnell
*Photo Research:* Carlotta Cooper

Photo credits:
Page 4 – Mary Evans Picture Library
Pages 7 (top) & 44 (top) – © 1995 – 2004 Denver Public Library, Colorado Historical Society and Denver Art Museum
Page 7 (bottom) – The Culture Archive
Pages 44 (bottom) & 45 (both) – Rex Features Ltd.

Library of Congress Cataloging-in-Publication Data

Jeffrey, Gary.
    Sitting Bull : the life of a Lakota Sioux chief / Gary Jeffrey and Kate Petty.—
1st ed.
    p. cm. — (Graphic nonfiction)
    Includes index.
    ISBN 1-4042-0247-1 (lib. bdg.)
    1. Sitting Bull, 1834?–1890—Juvenile literature. 2. Dakota Indians—Kings and rulers—Biography—Juvenile literature. 3. Hunkpapa Indians—Biography—Juvenile literature. 4. Little Bighorn, Battle of the, Mont., 1876—Juvenile literature. I. Petty, Kate. II. Title. III. Series.

    E99.D1J43 2005
    978.004'975244'0092—dc22

                                                                    2004005883

Manufactured in China

# CONTENTS

## WHO'S WHO

**Sitting Bull** (c. 1834–1890) Supreme chief of the Sioux Indians and a shaman. He fought the Americans for the freedom of his people and their sacred land.

**George Crook** (1828–1890) Known as Three Stars to the Indians, his job was to convince them to sell their land. Most of the Indians trusted him, even though he was the "greatest Indian fighter the army ever had."

**William Cody** (1846–1917) Better known as Buffalo Bill. He was an army scout and buffalo hunter before turning to the stage with his Wild West Show.

**White Bull** (1849–1954) The son of Sitting Bull's sister and a Miniconjou chief. He fought alongside the Hunkpapas. He lived a long time and left pictographs of his achievements. Some believe he killed Custer.

**Crazy Horse** (1842–1877) The fearless Oglala war chief who led the fight against Custer at Little Bighorn. He wore his hair loose and painted a lightning streak on his face.

**George Custer** (1839–1876) Young general of the U.S. 7th Cavalry who spent the last ten years of his life fighting the Native Americans.

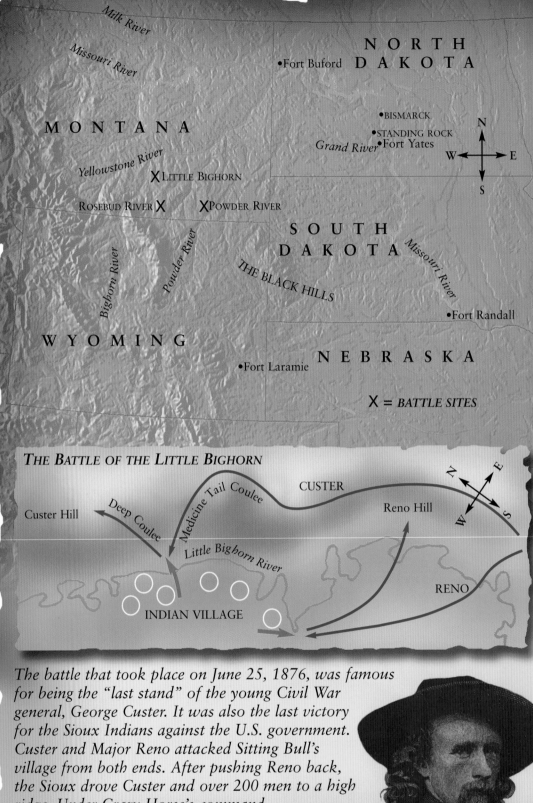

The battle that took place on June 25, 1876, was famous for being the "last stand" of the young Civil War general, George Custer. It was also the last victory for the Sioux Indians against the U.S. government. Custer and Major Reno attacked Sitting Bull's village from both ends. After pushing Reno back, the Sioux drove Custer and over 200 men to a high ridge. Under Crazy Horse's command, 3,000 warriors killed them all in a battle that lasted no more than two hours.

General Custer

# THE GREAT PLAINS

*T*he Great Plains cover almost a million square miles in the middle of North America. Until about 350 years ago, Native American tribes were the only people who lived there. They were hunters who lived in harmony with the land. They found everything they needed to live there.

### AN EXTREME CLIMATE
Far from the sea, the treeless grassy plains were very hot in summer and freezing cold in winter. They were filled with animals for food in the warmer months. In the snowy winter months, food became scarce. The Native Americans wore very little in the summer. They wrapped themselves in skins and blankets in cold weather.

### WHERE THE BUFFALO ROAM
Huge herds of buffalo crossed the plains in the millions during the summer. They provided the Native Americans with skins for clothing and shelter; bone and sinews for tools, utensils, and thread; fat for candles and soap, and meat for food. The Indians ate fresh meat in the summer but dried it for winter use. Before they had horses, the Native Americans dressed in animal skins to creep up unnoticed on the buffalo. They shot them with bows and arrows. Even with horses and guns, buffalo hunting was dangerous. It took great horse-riding skills and courage.

### BUFFALO HUNT!
*Indian hunters only killed as many buffalo as were needed. The women skinned and cut up the meat before loading it onto horses.*

# AN INDIAN NATION

*E*uropean explorers thought they
had arrived at the East Indies when
they set foot in North America. They
called the natives they met Indians. These
Native Americans had originally come from
Asia across Alaska about 12,000 years earlier.

## TRIBAL LANDS

There were many different Indian nations in
North America with different languages and
customs. They shared a great respect for the
natural world they lived in. Sea tribes of the
Northwest, like the Chinooks, made wooden huts,
canoes, and totem poles. The Iroquois Indians who
lived settled lives in the woodlands of the East had
a complex system of government. Plains Indians
like the Crow and Cheyenne were hunter
gatherers. Farther south, the Sioux tribes
were farmers as well as hunters.

## LAWFUL SOCIETY

*The laws made by the Iroquois in the Eastern
woodlands were based on democratic principles.*

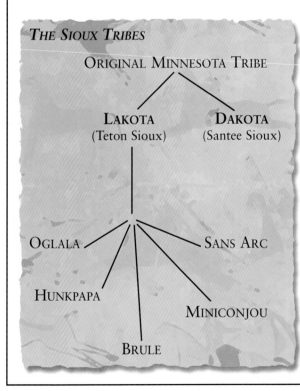

### THE SIOUX TRIBES

ORIGINAL MINNESOTA TRIBE

LAKOTA
(Teton Sioux)

DAKOTA
(Santee Sioux)

OGLALA

SANS ARC

HUNKPAPA

MINICONJOU

BRULE

### THE SIOUX NATION

Sioux means "snake." It was
the name given to Sioux
Indians by their enemies, the
Ojibwe. During the seventeenth
century, the Sioux people
migrated from Minnesota
across the Missouri River to
the Great Plains. They
separated into three language
groups – the Dakota, the
Lakota, and the Nakota, which
all mean "ally." Five tribes
made up the Lakota branch,
including Sitting Bull's tribe,
the Hunkpapa. For 150 years,
the Sioux Indians followed the
buffalo herds on the plains.

## THE DRIVE WESTWARD

The white people who came to America were often escaping poverty and hunger in their homelands. The West was a wilderness waiting to be farmed. The U.S. government encouraged people to move there. The tough pioneers hacked out homes from the forests to give their families a new start. The Gold Rush of 1849 brought miners hoping to make their fortunes. By 1869, the railroad had arrived to take even more people across the plains to the West.

## WHITE MAN'S INVASION

*In 1876, General Custer arrived in the Sioux Indians' sacred hills, the Paha Sapa. With him were a thousand gold prospectors hoping to make their fortune.*

## A MAN CALLED TATANKA-TYOTANKA

Sitting Bull, or Tatanka-Tyotanka, famous Sioux chief and shaman, was born around 1834. He was born in a place on the Grand River in present-day South Dakota known to the Indians as "Many Caches." His father and uncle were chiefs. Named "Slow" at first, he received his father's name at 14 after a daring feat in battle. Known as a peacemaker, in 1857 he became a tribal war chief. In 1869, he became Supreme Chief of the Sioux nation as war with the white man neared. He fought for the freedom of his people and was the "last Indian" to surrender to the U.S. government. He was killed in 1890.

## THE GREAT SIOUX CHIEF

*"In war he has no equal; in council he is superior to all; every word laid by him carries weight..." J.M. Walsh, a major in the Royal Canadian Mounted Police Force, on Sitting Bull in 1880.*

# SITTING BULL

## The Life of a Lakota Sioux Chief

SOUTH DAKOTA, 1834.

YEEEAH! YIP! YIP!

YIP!

FOR AS LONG AS THE SIOUX INDIANS COULD REMEMBER, THEIR PEOPLE HAD HUNTED *BUFFALO*.

BUFFALO PROVIDED THEM WITH EVERYTHING THEY NEEDED — FUR FOR WARM ROBES, SKIN FOR TEPEES, BONE FOR TOOLS, SINEW FOR BOWSTRINGS AND THREAD, AND OF COURSE...

...MEAT!

HERE YOU ARE.

THE BOY EXAMINED THE MEAT, WATCHED BY HIS UNCLE AND FATHER...

DOES JUMPING BADGER NOT **LIKE** BUFFALO MEAT?

HE DOES! BUT MY BOY LIKES TO TAKE HIS TIME AND **THINK** ABOUT IT FIRST.

THEN FROM NOW ON WE WILL CALL HIM **SLOW!**

SLOW WAS TAKEN UNDER HIS UNCLE'S WING. AS HE GREW UP, HE WAS TAUGHT THE WAYS OF THE HUNKPAPA TRIBE – THE ART OF **HUNTING**...

...AND WARFARE!

GOT YOU!

THE **COUP STICK** WAS A SYMBOL OF **BRAVERY.** THE HUNKPAPA THOUGHT IT WAS MUCH BRAVER TO TOUCH AN ENEMY WITH A COUP STICK THAN TO STRIKE HIM FROM A DISTANCE WITH AN ARROW.

SLOW WAS GOOD AT EVERYTHING HE DID. HE HAD THE MAKINGS OF A FINE WARRIOR. WHEN HE WAS 14, HE BEGAN PESTERING HIS FATHER TO BE ALLOWED TO GO OUT WITH A WAR PARTY...

ALL RIGHT! YOU MAY GO, BUT ONLY AS AN ERRAND BOY – NOTHING MORE.

THE WHITE EAGLE'S FEATHER WAS FOR BRAVERY. NOW THE BOY NEEDED TO EARN A RED FEATHER – FOR A WOUND. IT WAS NOT LONG IN COMING.

DURING A BATTLE WITH THE FLATHEADS, SITTING BULL MOUNTED UP...

I'M GOING TO TEST THEIR AIM!

FLISCH!

HA!

WHIZZZZ!

ZZZINGGG!

AS HE RETURNED...

YOUR FOOT!

IT'S NOTHING. JUST A SCRATCH!

THE WOUND WON SITTING BULL THE RED FEATHER AND HIGH HONOR WITHIN THE TRIBE. THE LAKOTA PRIZED STRENGTH AS HIGHLY AS COURAGE. FROM NOW ON, HE WOULD RIDE THE BEST PONIES. HE MADE SURE HE WAS AT THE FRONT IN EVERY BATTLE AND EVERY HUNT. SOON, SITTING BULL'S NAME WAS FAMOUS EVERYWHERE. WHEN HE WAS 20, HE MARRIED A WOMAN CALLED LIGHT HAIR.

12

MARRIAGE DID NOT MAKE THE YOUNG SITTING BULL ANY LESS DARING. FIVE YEARS LATER, IN A FIGHT WITH THE CROWS...

THE CROWS ARE GIVING UP!

WAIT! THEIR CHIEF WANTS TO DUEL SITTING BULL!

I ACCEPT!

EACH WARRIOR ADVANCED...

...AND PREPARED TO SHOOT...

CRACK!

BANG!

AAAGHHH!

THUNKK!

KRACK!

WHIZZZL

RIPPP!

PLOUGH!

SITTING BULL CLAIMED THE SCALP...

...AND A SECOND RED FEATHER. HE WOULD WALK WITH A LIMP FOREVER, BUT HE WAS BECOMING KNOWN AS ONE OF THE FINEST HUNKPAPA WARRIORS.

13

SITTING BULL WAS A BRILLIANT HUNTER AND A BRAVE WARRIOR. NOW, AT 25, HE WANTED TO BECOME A **WICHASHA WAKAN,** OR A SHAMAN.

DURING THAT SUMMER, THE HUNKPAPAS GATHERED ON THE EAST SIDE OF THE LITTLE MISSOURI RIVER FOR THEIR ANNUAL SUN DANCE CEREMONY.

THE DANCERS FASTED AND STARED AT THE SUN FOR DAYS. SITTING BULL HAD TO PERFORM A SPECIAL SACRIFICIAL SUN DANCE BEFORE HE COULD BECOME A WICHASHA WAKAN.

IT WAS CALLED THE PIERCING OF THE HEART. POINTED STICKS WERE INSERTED BENEATH THE MUSCLES OF HIS CHEST...

...HE WAS THEN HUNG FROM A POLE. SITTING BULL STARED INTO THE SUN AND PRAYED TO **WAKANTANKA** FOR HIS PEOPLE TO HAVE GOOD HEALTH AND PLENTIFUL FOOD.

*FINALLY,* HE TORE LOOSE.

I HEARD A VOICE...

...IT SAID WAKANTANKA GIVES YOU WHAT YOU ASK FOR. WAKANTANKA WILL GRANT YOUR WISH.

SITTING BULL WOULD DANCE MANY TIMES TO KNOW HIS PEOPLE AND WATANKA, THE GREAT MYSTERY. PEOPLE RESPECTED HIS HOLINESS. HE WAS ALSO GENEROUS AND KIND.

THE FOLLOWING YEAR, DEATH TOOK LIGHT HAIR AND AN INFANT SON. A FEW MONTHS LATER, SITTING BULL ADOPTED HIS NEPHEW, ONE BULL, TO RAISE AS HIS OWN.

HE WOULD TEACH ONE BULL THE WAYS OF THE WARRIOR. THE SAME YEAR, SITTING BULL WAS NOMINATED TO BECOME A TRIBAL WAR CHIEF, AN HONOR HE ACCEPTED GLADLY.

A FEW MONTHS LATER, SITTING BULL WAS LEADING A CHASE ON A GROUP OF HOHES.

WHOOP!

WHOOP!

YIP!

HE COUNTED FIRST COUP ONCE...

UGGH!

...AND THEN TWICE!

ARRRGH!

WHEN HE RETURNED TO DRY LAND...

WE'VE GOT A HOHE BOY!

LET'S KILL HIM!

SITTING BULL!

STOP!

GIVE HIM TO ME.

YOU MUST SPARE HIM!

HE WILL BE MY BROTHER!

THE BOY, KNOWN SIMPLY AS HOHE, JOINED ONE BULL AS AN ADOPTED MEMBER OF SITTING BULL'S FAMILY. IN TIME, HE TOO WOULD BECOME A FINE WARRIOR.

16

MEANWHILE, A FEW CROW WOMEN AND CHILDREN HAD BEEN TAKEN PRISONER...

YA-YIP!

KILL THEM ALL TO AVENGE JUMPING BULL!

NO!

IF YOU INTEND TO DO THIS FOR MY SAKE, TAKE CARE OF THEM AND LET THEM LIVE. MY FATHER WAS A BRAVE MAN. HE DIED A WARRIOR'S DEATH.

THE PRISONERS WERE SPARED.

FIGHTING WAS PART OF THE LAKOTA WAY OF LIFE.

IT WAS SAVAGE, BUT NOT WITHOUT KINDNESS. ABOVE ALL, THERE WAS HONOR. BUT LITTLE DID SITTING BULL AND HIS TRIBESMEN KNOW THAT THEIR WAY OF LIFE, AND THEIR VERY EXISTENCE, WAS ABOUT TO COME UNDER THREAT FROM WASICHU – THE WHITE MAN. SO FAR, THE ONLY WHITES THEY KNEW WERE THE TRADERS AND TRAPPERS AT OUTPOSTS LIKE FORT PIERRE.

JUST THREE YEARS AFTER JUMPING BULL'S DEATH, EVERYTHING WAS TO CHANGE. DURING THE 1850s, GOLD WAS DISCOVERED AT THE HEAD OF THE MISSOURI RIVER.

THIS WAS THE TERRITORY OF THEIR COUSINS, THE DAKOTA SIOUX, WHO ROSE UP AGAINST THE INVASION IN OUTRAGE.

HERE, ON THE NORTHERN PLAINS, THEY SOUGHT SAFETY WITH THEIR LAKOTA COUSINS. MEANWHILE, THE U.S. ARMY GATHERED A FORCE OF 5,000 SOLDIERS TO OCCUPY THE PLAINS AND CONQUER THE TRIBES.

IT BROUGHT THOUSANDS OF MINERS AND SETTLERS INTO THE LANDS EAST OF THE LAKOTAS.

THEIR REBELLION WAS SWIFTLY PUT DOWN BY U.S. GOVERNMENT FORCES. THE SURVIVORS FLED WEST.

THE STAGE WAS SET FOR A SHOWDOWN.

17

EARLY IN 1865, INDIAN MESSENGERS BROUGHT WORD TO SITTING BULL THAT A TERRIBLE THING HAD HAPPENED TO THE CHEYENNE INDIANS IN THE SOUTH...

THE VILLAGE WAS PEACEFUL BUT THE SOLDIERS KILLED THEM ALL...

...AND MUTILATED THEM!

...THEY ATTACKED THEM AS THEY SLEPT...

OVER 100 CHEYENNE WOMEN AND CHILDREN AND ABOUT 30 MEN WERE BUTCHERED IN THE SAND CREEK MASSACRE.

THE CHEYENNE SURVIVORS, INCLUDING CHIEF BLACK KETTLE, HAD FLED NORTH TO JOIN THE OGLALA TRIBE. RED CLOUD, THE OGLALA CHIEF, WOULD SOON BEGIN A WAR OF HIS OWN WITH THE SOLDIERS. MEANWHILE, THE HUNKPAPA HAD CONCERNS CLOSER TO HOME...

THAT SPRING, THE GOVERNMENT SOLDIERS BUSIED THEMSELVES BUILDING NEW FORTS IN THE LAKOTAS' TERRITORY. THE HUNKPAPA BUSIED THEMSELVES TRYING TO STOP THEM.

MONTH AFTER MONTH, THE LAKOTAS BURNED WOOD PILES, KILLED CATTLE, AND HOUNDED THE WORKERS AT THE FORTS. BUT THE BUILDINGS STILL WENT UP.

WHITE BULL AND A FEW OTHERS DECIDED TO TRAVEL SOUTH TO HELP THE OGLALAS IN THEIR WAR. AT THE END OF THE YEAR, CHEYENNE, ARAPAHO, AND SIOUX WARRIORS GATHERED TO PLAN A BIG ATTACK.

THEIR TARGET WAS FORT KEARNEY ON THE NORTH PLATTE RIVER. EARLY ONE DECEMBER DAY IN 1866, 2,000 OF THEM HID AROUND THE ROAD THAT LED TOWARD THE FORT.

A BAND OF WARRIORS SET OFF TO MAKE AN ATTACK ON THE FORT'S WOOD LODGE AS A TRICK TO DRAW OUT THE SOLDIERS.

IN 1868, RED CLOUD WON HIS WAR AGAINST THE FORTS. THE WHITES WERE PREPARED TO ALLOW THE OGLALA LANDS TO BE MADE INTO A SIOUX RESERVATION IN EXCHANGE FOR PEACE. THE WHITES INVITED THE NORTHERN TRIBES TO SIGN A TREATY AND COME TO LIVE ON THE RESERVATION. SITTING BULL'S FRIEND, **GALL**, WAS SENT TO MEET WITH THE WHITES. HE SIGNED THE TREATY WITHOUT KNOWING WHAT IT WOULD MEAN. MANY OF THE NORTHERN LAKOTAS WERE **UNHAPPY**.

THAT SAME YEAR, CHIEF FOUR HORNS CALLED A MEETING OF THE HUNKPAPA SHIRT WEARERS. *

WE HAVE ONLY THREE CHOICES. **FIRST**, WE GIVE IN TO THE WHITES, LIVE ON THEIR RESERVATION, AND TAKE THEIR CHARITY...

*FOUR EXPERIENCED MEN WHO CARRIED OUT TRIBAL DECISIONS.

...OR **SECOND**, WE TAKE WHAT CHARITY WE CAN FROM THE RESERVATION AGENCIES AND STILL HUNT THE BUFFALO ON OUR LANDS WHILE TRYING TO KEEP THE WHITES HAPPY...

...OR **THIRD**, WE REFUSE THE WHITES COMPLETELY, STICK WITH THE OLD WAYS, AND DO WHATEVER IT TAKES TO KEEP THEM OUT.

THE CHOICES WERE PUT BEFORE THE TRIBESPEOPLE. BY A MAJORITY VOTE THEY CHOSE THE **THIRD WAY**.

FOUR HORNS CALLED A **TRIBAL** MEETING. HE HAD AN ANNOUNCEMENT TO MAKE...

I'VE DECIDED TO STEP DOWN AS YOUR CHIEF. THERE ARE DIFFICULT TIMES AHEAD. THE THREAT TO OUR PEOPLE IS GREAT. A DIFFERENT KIND OF LEADERSHIP IS NEEDED...

...I PROPOSE THAT MY NEPHEW, CHIEF SITTING BULL, IS MADE CHIEF OF **ALL** THE HUNTING LAKOTAS!

THE LISTENERS AGREED. LATER THAT SUMMER IN A SPECIAL CEREMONY, SITTING BULL WAS MADE SUPREME CHIEF OF THE **SIOUX TRIBES**.

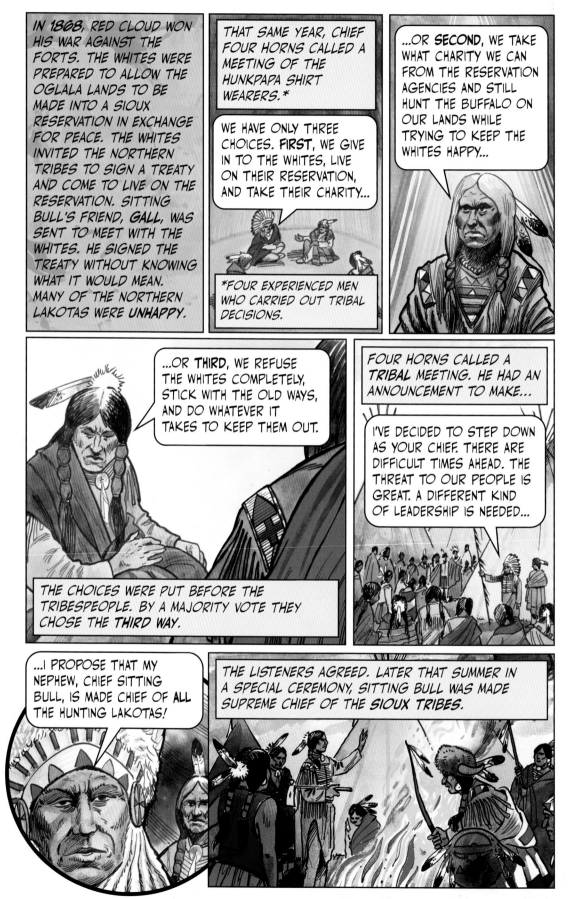

WHEN YOU TELL US TO FIGHT, WE'LL FIGHT! WHEN YOU TELL US TO MAKE PEACE, WE WILL MAKE PEACE!

THE PLAINS TRIBES WERE NOW DIVIDED INTO TWO GROUPS – AGENCY INDIANS AND HUNTING INDIANS. CRAZY HORSE COULD NEVER LIVE AS AN AGENCY INDIAN AND WITH OTHER OGLALAS HE DRIFTED NORTH TO JOIN THE HUNTERS.

THROUGHOUT 1870, SITTING BULL'S LAKOTAS CONTINUED TO HOUND THE FORTS IN THEIR TERRITORY. THAT AUTUMN THEY MOUNTED AN ATTACK ON THE CAMP AT FORT BUFORD...

INDIANS!

HURRY! INTO THE SHED!

WHERE'S CHARLIE?

CHARLES TECK HAD BEEN CAUGHT IN THE OPEN...

BANG! BANG!

BANG!

CLICK!

WHACK!

NNNGHH!

STAB!

AAAAGHHH!

THE WHITE BOY FOUGHT BRAVELY, IT WILL BE AN HONOR TO TAKE THIS...

BEFORE THEY LEFT, THE LAKOTAS SALUTED THE WHITE MEN...

AAYAAH!

YIP! YIP! YIP!

WHAT THE – ? IT'S CHARLIE'S SCALP!

HEY! WHAT'S THAT HE'S HOLDING?

TURNING AWAY FROM THE FORTS, SITTING BULL SPENT THE NEXT TWO YEARS WAGING WAR AGAINST RIVAL TRIBES. IN THE SPRING OF 1872, OVER 2,000 OF HIS WARRIORS HAD GATHERED FOR AN ATTACK ON A CROW CAMP AT THE YELLOWSTONE RIVER. *SCOUTS* WERE SENT OUT THE PREVIOUS DAY. THEY CAME BACK WITH NEWS THAT A CAMP OF SOLDIERS HAD BEEN DISCOVERED IN THE *NEXT VALLEY*.

SITTING BULL AND CRAZY HORSE WENT TO LOOK. IT WAS A GROUP OF CAVALRY GUARDING GOVERNMENT ENGINEERS. THE ENGINEERS WERE SURVEYING A ROUTE FOR A NEW RAILROAD...

HOW DARE THEY COME HERE! WE FOUGHT THE CROWS FOR THIS LAND. IT'S OURS!

THEY DECIDED TO *ATTACK*.

THOUGH FEW IN NUMBER, THE SOLDIERS WERE WELL ARMED. THEY KEPT THE INDIANS AWAY BY FIRING AT THEM.

AT THE HEIGHT OF THE ACTION, SITTING BULL GOT HIS PIPE.

FZZZZ!

ZING!!

PTANGG!

PEEEEOW!

ZING!!

THOSE WHO WISH TO SMOKE WITH ME – COME!

ONLY FOUR WERE BRAVE ENOUGH...

ZING!!

WINNG!

SPUTT!

PFUT!

...AND THEY SAT UNTIL THE TOBACCO WAS FINISHED.

24

SITTING BULL CALLED OFF THE ATTACK AND THE ENGINEERS WENT HOME. THE NEXT YEAR, MORE SOLDIERS RETURNED. THEY WERE LED BY A COMMANDER THAT THE LAKOTAS NAMED "LONG HAIR." WHITE MEN KNEW HIM AS **CUSTER**.

LONG HAIR WAS A FEARLESS WARRIOR. WHEN THE INDIANS ATTACKED HIS PARTY, HE DROVE THEM OFF. HE CHASED THEM BACK OVER THE YELLOWSTONE RIVER.

IN 1874, LONG HAIR RETURNED TO THE HEARTLAND OF THE SIOUX COUNTRY, *PAHA SAPA*, OR **THE BLACK HILLS**. HE BROUGHT SURVEYORS AND PROSPECTORS **LOOKING FOR GOLD**. THE SIOUX WERE ALARMED. THEY KNEW THAT THE MOUNTAINS WERE FULL OF THE YELLOW METAL. WHEN IT WAS DISCOVERED, THE WHITES WOULD ARRIVE AND SWARM OVER THEIR SACRED HILLS TO DIG IT UP.

THE NEXT SUMMER, THE CHEYENNES JOINED THE SIOUX AT THEIR ANNUAL SUN DANCE. SITTING BULL CALLED FOR **TWO PIPES** TO BE FILLED AND BROUGHT FORTH...

...ONE REPRESENTING THE **SIOUX**, THE OTHER REPRESENTING THE **CHEYENNES**.

THEN HE DANCED...

WE NEARLY HAVE THEM...

WE...

...HAVE THEM!

THE GREAT SPIRIT HAS GIVEN OUR ENEMIES TO US. BUT WE DO NOT YET KNOW **WHO** THEY ARE...

**WHOEVER** THE ENEMIES TURNED OUT TO BE, THE CHEYENNES **VOWED** TO FIGHT ALONGSIDE THEIR SIOUX BROTHERS TO DEFEAT THEM.

THE PROMISE OF GOLD BROUGHT THOUSANDS OF PROSPECTORS TO THE **BLACK HILLS**. BUT SEVEN YEARS EARLIER, THE **U.S. GOVERNMENT** HAD GIVEN THESE LANDS TO THE SIOUX AS A HUNTING GROUND. WHITES WERE FORBIDDEN TO TRESPASS ON IT. THE GOVERNMENT DECIDED TO MEET WITH THE CHIEFS AND OFFER TO **BUY** THE HILLS FROM THEM.

SITTING BULL REFUSED TO GO. CRAZY HORSE SENT HIS LIEUTENANT, LITTLE-BIG-MAN, WITH A BAND OF OGLALA WARRIORS, TO STATE **HIS** POSITION AT THE MEETING....

I, LITTLE-BIG-MAN, WILL **KILL** ANY CHIEF WHO SPEAKS UP FOR SELLING THE BLACK HILLS!

**LONE HORN**, THE MINICONJOUS CHIEF, CAME TO SEE SITTING BULL AFTER THE MEETING...

THE AGENCY CHIEFS WERE READY TO SIGN! I SAID "YOU ARE VERY **CHEAP!**"

YES, BROTHER!

THESE HILLS ARE A **TREASURE** FOR US...

THEY ARE OUR SOURCE OF **FOOD!** WHEN THE PEOPLE HAVE **NOTHING** TO EAT, WE CAN ALL GO THERE AND **GET** SOMETHING TO EAT.

AS FAR AS THE HUNTING BANDS WERE CONCERNED, **PAHA SAPA** WAS NOT FOR SALE...AT ANY PRICE.

THE INDIANS **REFUSED** THE GOVERNMENT'S OFFER AND SETTLED DOWN IN THEIR WINTER CAMPS. THE WEATHER HAD TURNED VERY HARSH AND SITTING BULL WAS SURPRISED WHEN A RUNNER APPEARED THROUGH THE SNOW. HE WAS BRINGING A **MESSAGE** FROM THE RESERVATION AGENCY...

YOU ARE TO BRING YOUR PEOPLE ONTO THE RESERVATION BY THE END OF THE MONTH – OR THE SOLDIERS WILL COME.

SITTING BULL, WE CANNOT GO. OUR PONIES WOULD FREEZE!

TELL THEM WE CAN DO **NOTHING** UNTIL THE GRASS BECOMES GREEN. **THEN** WE WILL SEE.

IT WAS SPRING 1876 WHEN A MIXED GROUP OF CHEYENNES AND SIOUX DECIDED TO CAMP OFF-RESERVATION NEAR THE POWDER RIVER AND SEARCH FOR GAME.

THE CHEYENNE CHIEF, HOLY MAN ICE, WAS STIRRING WHEN...

CRASH! BANG!

BANG! *BANG!* SHRIEEEK!

?

*PHWEEEEEOW!*

!

SOLDIERS!

CRACK! CRACK! CRACK!

AAAGH!

LEAVING EVERYTHING BEHIND THEM, THE SURVIVORS FLED ACROSS THE POWDER RIVER.

27

FREEZING AND HUNGRY, THEY SOUGHT SAFETY AT CRAZY HORSE'S VILLAGE UPRIVER...

MY FRIENDS, I CANNOT FEED YOU ALL. WE MUST GO TO SITTING BULL.

AT SITTING BULL'S CAMP, THEY WERE GIVEN EVERYTHING THEY NEEDED.

THE CHIEF CALLED A WAR COUNCIL...

WE ARE NOT LOOKING FOR A FIGHT WITH THESE SOLDIERS.

WE MUST WORK TOGETHER, ALL THE TRIBES, AND SCARE OFF THE SOLDIERS.

ONE BY ONE, THE HUNTING BANDS JOINED SITTING BULL'S GROUP TO FOLLOW THE BUFFALO. THEN ONE MORNING, THE CHIEF SLIPPED AWAY TO THINK ABOUT THINGS ALONE WITH WAKANTANKA. HE FELL ASLEEP...

WHEN HE RETURNED, HE CALLED HIS PEOPLE TOGETHER...

MY FRIENDS, I HAD A DREAM...

I SAW A GREAT DUST STORM COMING, FROM THE EAST...

...AND FROM THE WEST, A PURE WHITE CLOUD SAILING SMOOTHLY...

...BEHIND THE DUST STORM WERE MANY SOLDIERS. THE STORM CRASHED INTO THE WHITE CLOUD AND TRIED TO CONSUME IT...

CRAAACK!

...WHEN THE LIGHTNING WAS OVER, THE DUST STORM WAS GONE! ONLY THE WHITE CLOUD REMAINED.

THE MEANING WAS CLEAR. SOLDIERS WERE COMING FROM THE EAST TO DESTROY THE VILLAGE – BUT THEY WOULD FAIL.

A MONTH LATER, THE HUNKPAPA HELD THEIR SUN DANCE FESTIVAL.

THE PEOPLE FROM THE OTHER TRIBES LOOKED ON AS SITTING BULL MADE A SACRIFICE...

HIS BROTHER, HOHE, STAYED WITH HIM.

TOGETHER THEY DANCED AND PRAYED...

...VISIONS CAME...

...AND A VOICE SPOKE...

THESE SOLDIERS DO NOT POSSESS EARS. THEY ARE TO DIE, BUT YOU ARE NOT TO TAKE THEIR THINGS.

WHILE SITTING BULL RESTED, BLACK MOON RELATED THE MEANING OF THE VISION...

WAKANTANKA WILL GIVE US A GREAT VICTORY OVER THE SOLDIERS. WE WILL KILL THEM ALL! BUT IN RETURN, WE MUST NOT STEAL FROM THEIR BODIES.

A WEEK LATER, NEAR THE ROSEBUD RIVER, INDIAN FORCES MANAGED TO DRIVE AWAY AN ARMY COMMANDED BY GEORGE CROOK, CALLED THREE STARS. IT WAS A GREAT VICTORY, BUT NO ONE BELIEVED IT WAS THE BATTLE IN SITTING BULL'S DREAM. THAT WAS YET TO COME. MEANWHILE, THE LARGE CAMP MOVED SLOWLY UP THE BIGHORN VALLEY IN SEARCH OF ANTELOPE.

THEY SET UP THEIR TEPEES NEAR A STREAM KNOWN AS THE GREASY GRASS.*

*THE LITTLE BIGHORN.

THE TEPEE VILLAGE WAS THE BIGGEST EVER ASSEMBLED. BUT PEOPLE COULD ONLY CAMP FOR A FEW DAYS BEFORE THE GRASS AND THE TIMBER WERE USED UP. MEANWHILE, CAMP LIFE WENT ON...

...THE WOMEN MADE NEW LODGEPOLES FOR THEIR TEPEES AND CURED FRESH BUFFALO HIDES TO MAKE CLOTHING AND LODGE COVERINGS...

HUNKPAPA

MINICONJOU

BLACKFEET

SANS ARCS

BRULE

OGLALA

CHEYENNE

...WHILE THE MEN RELAXED BETWEEN HUNTS, SMOKED, AND TOLD EACH OTHER GREAT TALES OF BRAVERY, OLD AND NEW.

IN THE *HUNKPAPA CIRCLE*, SITTING BULL WAS UNEASY...

ONE BULL! COME, WE ARE TO MAKE A SACRIFICE.

WAKANTANKA, PITY ME. I OFFER YOU THIS PEACE PIPE. WE WANT TO LIVE. GUARD US AGAINST ALL MISFORTUNES. PLEASE PITY ME...

LONG HAIR?

IT WAS CUSTER! OGLALA AND MINICONJOU WARRIORS FROM THE VILLAGE HAD DRIVEN HIS CHARGE UPHILL. THERE, CUSTER MADE A *STAND*...

WHITE BULL LED A CHARGE ON *CUSTER'S* MEN...

THE HORSES *STAMPEDED*... BANG!

NOW THE SOLDIERS WERE *HERDED* LIKE BUFFALO...

AAAGGGHH!

...AND *SLAUGHTERED*.

*CRAZY HORSE* HAD ARRIVED! TOGETHER, HE AND WHITE BULL *CHARGED* AT THE *SOLDIERS*, SPLITTING THEM IN TWO GROUPS.

ONE GROUP *FLED*.

THE INDIANS PICKED THEM OFF *ONE BY ONE*.

THE SECOND GROUP MADE A BRAVE *LAST STAND*...

THE INDIANS KILLED THEM ALL.

*LONG HAIR* WAS AMONG THEM.

33

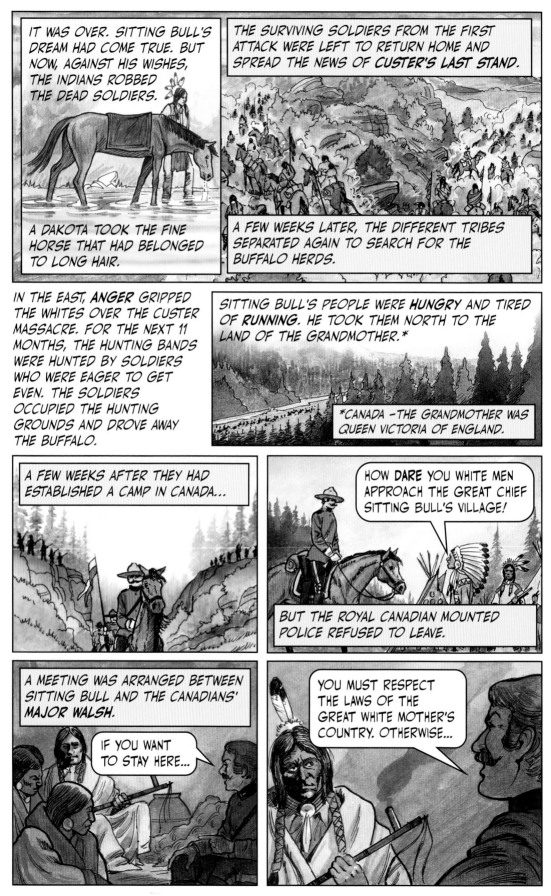

IT WAS OVER. SITTING BULL'S DREAM HAD COME TRUE. BUT NOW, AGAINST HIS WISHES, THE INDIANS ROBBED THE DEAD SOLDIERS.

A DAKOTA TOOK THE FINE HORSE THAT HAD BELONGED TO LONG HAIR.

THE SURVIVING SOLDIERS FROM THE FIRST ATTACK WERE LEFT TO RETURN HOME AND SPREAD THE NEWS OF **CUSTER'S LAST STAND**.

A FEW WEEKS LATER, THE DIFFERENT TRIBES SEPARATED AGAIN TO SEARCH FOR THE BUFFALO HERDS.

IN THE EAST, **ANGER** GRIPPED THE WHITES OVER THE CUSTER MASSACRE. FOR THE NEXT 11 MONTHS, THE HUNTING BANDS WERE HUNTED BY SOLDIERS WHO WERE EAGER TO GET EVEN. THE SOLDIERS OCCUPIED THE HUNTING GROUNDS AND DROVE AWAY THE BUFFALO.

SITTING BULL'S PEOPLE WERE **HUNGRY** AND TIRED OF **RUNNING**. HE TOOK THEM NORTH TO THE LAND OF THE GRANDMOTHER.*

*CANADA —THE GRANDMOTHER WAS QUEEN VICTORIA OF ENGLAND.

A FEW WEEKS AFTER THEY HAD ESTABLISHED A CAMP IN CANADA...

HOW **DARE** YOU WHITE MEN APPROACH THE GREAT CHIEF SITTING BULL'S VILLAGE!

BUT THE ROYAL CANADIAN MOUNTED POLICE REFUSED TO LEAVE.

A MEETING WAS ARRANGED BETWEEN SITTING BULL AND THE CANADIANS' **MAJOR WALSH**.

IF YOU WANT TO STAY HERE...

YOU MUST RESPECT THE LAWS OF THE GREAT WHITE MOTHER'S COUNTRY. OTHERWISE...

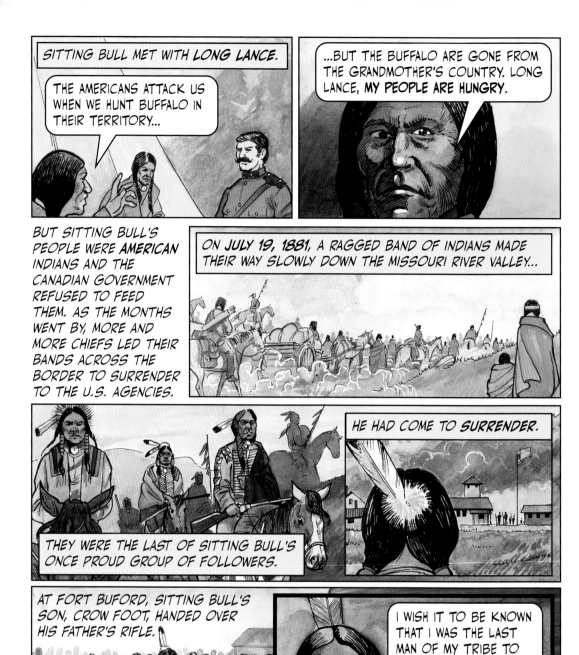

SITTING BULL MET WITH **LONG LANCE**.

THE AMERICANS ATTACK US WHEN WE HUNT BUFFALO IN THEIR TERRITORY...

...BUT THE BUFFALO ARE GONE FROM THE GRANDMOTHER'S COUNTRY. LONG LANCE, **MY PEOPLE ARE HUNGRY**.

BUT SITTING BULL'S PEOPLE WERE **AMERICAN** INDIANS AND THE CANADIAN GOVERNMENT REFUSED TO FEED THEM. AS THE MONTHS WENT BY, MORE AND MORE CHIEFS LED THEIR BANDS ACROSS THE BORDER TO SURRENDER TO THE U.S. AGENCIES.

ON **JULY 19, 1881**, A RAGGED BAND OF INDIANS MADE THEIR WAY SLOWLY DOWN THE MISSOURI RIVER VALLEY...

THEY WERE THE LAST OF SITTING BULL'S ONCE PROUD GROUP OF FOLLOWERS.

HE HAD COME TO **SURRENDER**.

AT FORT BUFORD, SITTING BULL'S SON, CROW FOOT, HANDED OVER HIS FATHER'S RIFLE.

I WISH IT TO BE KNOWN THAT I WAS THE LAST MAN OF MY TRIBE TO SURRENDER MY RIFLE.

MY SON HAS GIVEN IT TO YOU, AND **NOW** HE WANTS TO KNOW **HOW** HE IS GOING TO MAKE A LIVING.

A FEW DAYS LATER, A SHIP, THE GENERAL SHERMAN, ARRIVED TO TAKE SITTING BULL AND HIS PEOPLE UPRIVER TO **BISMARCK**, NORTH DAKOTA, WHERE THEY WERE TO BE RECEIVED BY THE TOWN'S LEADERS.

SITTING BULL WAS SURPRISED BY THE LARGE CROWDS THAT GREETED THEM.

THE ONCE FRIGHTENING SIOUX LEADER HAD TURNED INTO **A CURIOSITY.**

AFTER A BRIEF IMPRISONMENT, HIS BAND WAS RELEASED TO THE STANDING ROCK AGENCY ON THE GREAT SIOUX RESERVATION. THERE HE WOULD LIVE OUT THE REST OF HIS DAYS. BUT LIFE WAS FAR FROM QUIET AND THE CHIEF RECEIVED MANY VISITORS...

...SIGNED **AUTOGRAPHS...**

...AND EVEN HAD HIS **PORTRAIT PAINTED.**

A FEW MONTHS LATER, HE WENT TO BISMARCK. HE WAS A GUEST SPEAKER AT THE CEREMONY TO DRIVE IN THE LAST SPIKE ON THE **NORTHERN PACIFIC RAILROAD.**

...AND INTRODUCING THE OLDEST PURE DAKOTA LIVING HERE AT PRESENT... CHIEF **SITTING BULL!**

SITTING BULL REALIZED THAT IN THIS STRANGE WHITE WORLD HE HAD BECOME **A CELEBRITY.**

HIS SPEECH WAS A GREAT SUCCESS.

LATER, HE WENT WITH OTHER SIOUX CHIEFS TO STAGE SHOWS IN NEW YORK AND PHILADELPHIA.

ON **JUNE 6, 1885,** A CONTRACT WAS MADE WITH THE GOVERNMENT'S INDIAN OFFICE FOR SITTING BULL TO APPEAR FOR ONE SEASON IN WILLIAM CODY'S FAMOUS **WILD WEST SHOW.**

THOUSANDS CAME. EVERYONE WANTED TO SEE **"THE SLAYER OF CUSTER"** FOR THEMSELVES.

PART CIRCUS AND PART THEATER, THE SHOW FEATURED RE-CREATIONS OF FRONTIER LIFE USING ANIMALS AND PEOPLE.

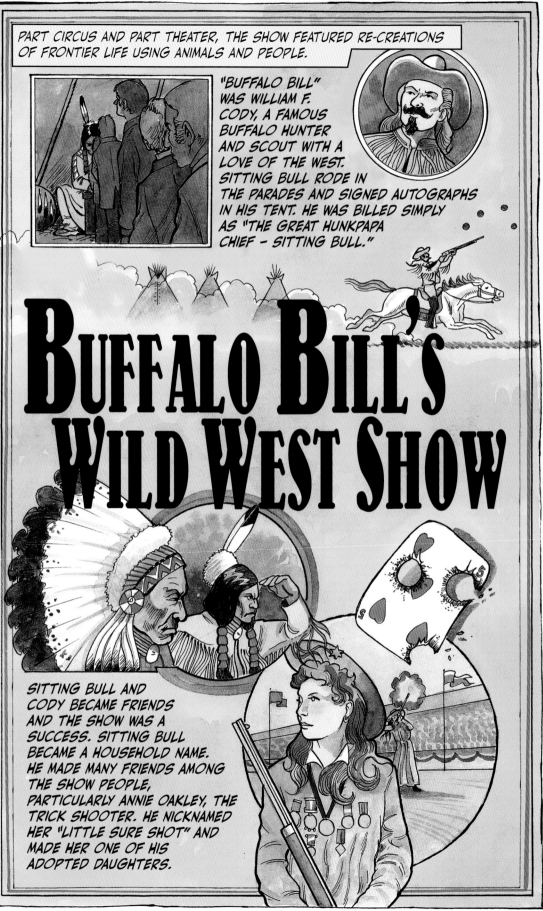

"BUFFALO BILL" WAS WILLIAM F. CODY, A FAMOUS BUFFALO HUNTER AND SCOUT WITH A LOVE OF THE WEST. SITTING BULL RODE IN THE PARADES AND SIGNED AUTOGRAPHS IN HIS TENT. HE WAS BILLED SIMPLY AS "THE GREAT HUNKPAPA CHIEF – SITTING BULL."

# BUFFALO BILL'S WILD WEST SHOW

SITTING BULL AND CODY BECAME FRIENDS AND THE SHOW WAS A SUCCESS. SITTING BULL BECAME A HOUSEHOLD NAME. HE MADE MANY FRIENDS AMONG THE SHOW PEOPLE, PARTICULARLY ANNIE OAKLEY, THE TRICK SHOOTER. HE NICKNAMED HER "LITTLE SURE SHOT" AND MADE HER ONE OF HIS ADOPTED DAUGHTERS.

AT THE END OF THE TOUR, SITTING BULL HAD TO RETURN TO STANDING ROCK. BEFORE THE SIOUX CHIEF LEFT, WILLIAM CODY THANKED HIM WARMLY AND PRESENTED HIM WITH A *CIRCUS PONY*...

...AND A *WHITE HAT*.

IT WAS TIME TO SETTLE BACK INTO RESERVATION LIFE, BUT THERE WAS *TROUBLE* AHEAD...

...WITH AGENCY BOSS, *JAMES MCLAUGHLIN*.

IT'S *TOO BAD!*

HE'S NOT EVEN A *REAL* CHIEF ANY MORE. YET HE WANTS TO *BLOCK EVERYTHING* I TRY TO DO FOR HIS PEOPLE!

SITTING BULL SAW IT DIFFERENTLY...

RED CLOUD! SPOTTED TAIL! ALL THOSE "AGENCY" CHIEFS...

...THEY'RE TOO QUICK TO GIVE UP THE OLD WAYS AND TO LET THE WHITES TURN US INTO *WHITE FARMERS!*

SITTING BULL AND MCLAUGHLIN BATTLED FOR THE HEARTS AND MINDS OF THE SIOUX NATION. LIFE AT STANDING ROCK CONTINUED AS NORMAL.

WITH FOOD BEING RATIONED...

GROWING CROPS...

...AND EVERY TWO WEEKS, *KILLING DAY,* WHEN ANIMALS WERE KILLED FOR FOOD.

CRACK!

IT WAS NOT THE *WILD* AND *FREE* LIFE HIS PEOPLE HAD ONCE ENJOYED, BUT THE OLD SIOUX CHIEF CONTENTED HIMSELF WITH THE THOUGHT THAT THINGS COULD BE MUCH *WORSE.* AS INDEED, THEY WOULD TURN OUT TO BE...

39

THE GREAT SIOUX RESERVATION WAS A FRACTION OF THE INDIANS' ORIGINAL TERRITORY BUT IT WAS STILL 35,000 SQUARE MILES OF LAND. IMMIGRANTS FROM EASTERN EUROPE WERE POURING INTO THE EAST DAKOTA REGION. THEY LOOKED AT ALL THAT LAND WITH HUNGRY EYES.

THE U.S. GOVERNMENT DECIDED IT WAS TIME TO CARVE IT UP. THEY SENT THREE STARS CROOK AND A COMMISSION TO CONVINCE THE INDIANS TO SELL...

THE WHITE MEN IN THE EAST ARE LIKE BIRDS...

...THEY ARE HATCHING OUT OF THEIR EGGS EVERY YEAR AND THERE IS NOT ENOUGH ROOM FOR THEM...

...THEY SEE A BIG BODY OF LAND YOU ARE NOT USING AND THEY WANT THE LAND!

THOUGH HE WAS AN OLD ENEMY, MOST OF THE INDIANS TRUSTED THREE STARS...

...BUT SITTING BULL DID NOT. WHEN THE COMMISSION FINALLY CAME TO STANDING ROCK HE FOUND HIMSELF BARRED FROM THE PROCEEDINGS...

LET ME THROUGH!

OUR LAND IS THE MOST VALUABLE POSSESSION WE HAVE. IT IS FOR OUR CHILDREN! LET US STAND AS ONE FAMILY, AS WE DID BEFORE THE WHITE PEOPLE LED US ASTRAY!

BUT IT WAS TOO LATE. THE CHIEFS HAD ALREADY AGREED TO SIGN.

AS SITTING BULL WALKED AWAY, A JOURNALIST STOPPED HIM...

HOW DO THE INDIANS FEEL ABOUT GIVING UP THEIR LANDS?

INDIANS?

40

THERE ARE **NO** INDIANS LEFT BUT **ME!**

THEY COULD NO LONGER **HUNT** OR PRACTICE THEIR **RELIGION,** AND NOW THEIR LAND WAS GONE.

HIS PEOPLE WERE BEATEN AND ALMOST WITHOUT HOPE. TO ADD TO THESE WOES, THE CROPS BEGAN TO FAIL. THE GOVERNMENT DECIDED TO CUT THEIR RATIONS.

STARVATION LOOMED.

THEN WORD CAME OF A **NEW INDIAN RELIGION** THAT HAD TAKEN HOLD OF THE TRIBES IN THE FAR WEST...

LAKOTAS FROM THE OTHER RESERVATIONS WENT TO NEVADA TO INVESTIGATE. THEY RETURNED WITH TALES OF A NEW INDIAN SHAMAN CALLED WOVOKA. WOVOKA TOLD HIS PEOPLE TO DANCE FOR THE COMING DAY WHEN...

...A GREAT WEIGHT OF EARTH WOULD COVER THE LAND. THE BELIEVERS WOULD BE LIFTED ABOVE, AS THE SOIL BURIED THE WHITE PEOPLE BELOW. THE DANCERS' ANCESTORS WOULD RETURN. BUFFALO AND GAME WOULD BE PLENTIFUL ON THE PLAINS AGAIN. BUT ONLY IF THEY DANCED...

...THE GHOST DANCE.

THE LAKOTA TRAVELED FROM AGENCY TO AGENCY, TEACHING PEOPLE THE DANCE. IT SPREAD LIKE WILDFIRE.

SITTING BULL'S HUNKPAPAS ABANDONED THEIR CABINS. THEY ERECTED A LODGE VILLAGE ABOVE HIS FARM, WHERE THEY WOULD DANCE THEMSELVES INTO A TRANCE-LIKE STATE AND TALK TO THE DEAD.

AGENCY BOSS MCLAUGHLIN WAS **ALARMED**...

THIS **EXTREME** RELIGION HAS NO PLACE HERE. THESE PEOPLE STAND ON THE THRESHOLD OF CIVILIZATION...

...THE DANCING MUST BE **STOPPED**!

SITTING BULL REFUSED TO STOP THEM. HE WAS STILL A WICHASHA WAKAN. HE HAD A RESPONSIBILITY TO HIS PEOPLE TO HELP THEM IN **ANY** SPIRITUAL QUEST.

THE SIOUX RESERVATIONS WERE NOW SURROUNDED ON ALL SIDES BY NEW WHITE SETTLEMENTS. AS WORD OF THE DANCING SPREAD, THE SETTLERS BECAME **CRAZY WITH FEAR**. THEY THOUGHT THAT THE INDIANS WERE ABOUT TO RISE UP AND **SLAY THEM**.

SITTING BULL WAS THE FIGUREHEAD OF **INDIAN RESISTANCE**. THE U.S. GOVERNMENT DECIDED THAT HIS ARREST AND IMPRISONMENT WAS THE BEST SOLUTION TO THE CRISIS.

DAYBREAK, DECEMBER 15, 1890 – SITTING BULL'S CABIN.

SITTING BULL!

LET GO OF ME! I'LL GO WITHOUT ANY ASSISTANCE!

# THE END OF THE SIOUX?

*T*he battle at Wounded Knee that took place soon after Sitting Bull's death marked the end of the Indian resistance. "A people's dream died here," said one survivor.

## DEATH IN THE SNOW
*The bodies of the Indians killed at Wounded Knee were left in the snow. When survivors came to bury them, they found Big Foot frozen like this.*

## THE BATTLE OF WOUNDED KNEE
With Sitting Bull dead, many Hunkpapas set off with the Miniconjou chief, Big Foot, to Pine Ridge and the protection of Red Cloud. Traveling in the freezing cold, Big Foot became sick. Before long, the army picked up the travelers and took them to the army camp at Wounded Knee Creek. They arrived at night. At first, the soldiers treated them kindly, giving extra tents and a stove for the sick Big Foot. But in the morning, a fight broke out over a hidden rifle. Suddenly the soldiers were firing on all the Indians, shooting into the tepees. Big Foot and nearly 300 of the 350 Indians were killed.

## A SYMBOL OF STRENGTH
*In death as well as life, Sitting Bull became a symbol of resistance and the determination to fight for his people and their way of life.*

### THE SIOUX TODAY

Today 30,000 Sioux Indians live on reservations in South Dakota and on smaller ones in North Dakota, Nebraska, Montana, and Canada. Many Sioux have left the reservations to find work in the cities. For many, reservation life is very difficult. Some Sioux are starting to raise buffalo herds again and are bringing back some of the old traditions.

*RESERVATION LIFE*
*Some modern Native Americans still live in traditional villages with no running water or electricity.*

*MODERN CHIEF*
*Today, Indian culture and craft is much admired.*

# GLOSSARY

**agencies** U.S. government groups responsible for managing the Native American reservations.

**ancestors** Members of a person's family who lived a long time ago.

**artillery** Soldiers who use large, powerful guns that are mounted on wheels or tracks.

**avenge** To get back at someone who has done something wrong to you.

**cavalry** Soldiers on horseback.

**celebrity** A famous person, especially an entertainer.

**commission** A group of people who meet to solve a problem.

**coup stick** A stick used by the Lakota to touch an enemy, an honor higher than killing that enemy.

**curiosity** Something unusual or strange.

**Lakota** A plains tribe that spoke the Sioux language.

**migrate** To move from one place to another.

**mutilate** To injure someone seriously.

**pictographs** Painted images used to tell a story.

**prospectors** People who search for something valuable, such as gold.

**ration** To give out in limited amounts; a limited amount, especially of food.

**reservation** Lands given to Native Americans by the U.S. government on which to live.

**shaman** A person who acts as a contact between an invisible spirit world and the visible world and who heals the sick and forecasts events.

**sinew** A strong tissue taken from buffalo and used as string.

**slaughter** The brutal killings of large numbers of people.

**stampede** To make a sudden, wild rush in one direction.

**survey** To measure an area in order to make a map or plan.

**trance-like** Being awake but not really aware of what is happening around you.

**trespass** To enter someone's property without permission.

**Wakantanka** The Holy Spirit.

**war council** A group that discusses plans for war.

**Wasichu** The white man.

**Wichasha wakan** A holy man.

# FOR MORE INFORMATION

## ORGANIZATIONS

Wounded Knee: The Museum
207 Tenth Avenue
P.O. Box 348
Wall, SD 57790
(970) 226-3218
Web site: http://www.woundedkneemuseum.org/

The Sioux Indian Museum
222 New York Street
Rapid City, SD 57701
(605) 394-6923
Web site: http://www.journeymuseum.org/english/thecollections/sioux

## FOR FURTHER READING

Brash, Sarah, ed. *The Defiant Chiefs*. Boston, MA: Time-Life Inc., 1999.

Donovan, Jim. *Custer and the Little Bighorn: The Man, The Mystery, The Myth*. Stillwater, MN: Voyageur Press Inc., 2001.

Iannone, Catherine. *Sitting Bull: Lakota Leader*. Danbury, CT: Scholastic Library Publishing, 1999.

Kretzer-Malvehy, Terry. *Passage to Little Bighorn*. Madison, WI: Turtleback Books, 1999.

Schleichert, Elizabeth. *Sitting Bull: Sioux Leader*. Berkeley Heights, NJ: Enslow Publishers, Inc., 1997.

# INDEX

## Web Sites

Due to the changing nature of Internet links, the Rosen Publishing Group, Inc., has developed an online list of Web sites related to the subject of this book. This site is updated regularly. Please use this link to access the list:

http://www.rosenlinks.com/gnf/bull